PLYMOUTH COMMERCIAL VEHICLES

PHOTO ARCHIVE

Jim Benjaminson

Iconografix
Photo Archive Series

Iconografix
PO Box 446
Hudson, Wisconsin 54016 USA

Library of Congress Card Number: 99-71748

ISBN 1-58388-004-6

99 00 01 02 03 04 05 5 4 3 2 1

Printed in the United States of America

Cover and book design by Shawn Glidden

Edited by Dylan Frautschi

Iconografix Inc. exists to preserve history through the publication of notable photographic archives and the list of titles under the Iconografix imprint is constantly growing. Transportation enthusiasts should be on the Iconografix mailing list and are invited to write and ask for a catalog, free of charge.

Authors and editors in the field of transportation history are invited to contact the Editorial Department at Iconografix, Inc., PO Box 446, Hudson, WI 54016. We require a minimum of 120 photographs per subject. We prefer subjects narrow in focus, e.g., a specific model, railroad, or racing venue. Photographs must be of high-quality, suited to large format reproduction.

PREFACE

The histories of machines and mechanical gadgets are contained in the books, journals, correspondence, and personal papers stored in libraries and archives throughout the world. Written in tens of languages, covering thousands of subjects, the stories are recorded in millions of words.

Words are powerful. Yet, the impact of a single image, a photograph or an illustration, often relates more than dozens of pages of text. Fortunately, many of the libraries and archives that house the words also preserve the images.

In the *Photo Archive Series,* Iconografix reproduces photographs and illustrations selected from public and private collections. The images are chosen to tell a story—to capture the character of their subject. Reproduced as found, they are accompanied by the captions made available by the archive.

The Iconografix *Photo Archive Series* is dedicated to young and old alike, the enthusiast, the collector and anyone who, like us, is fascinated by "things" mechanical.

ACKNOWLEDGMENTS

Cover photo courtesy Willard and Della Stein

Special thanks to: Don Bunn, Earl C. Buton, Jr., Chrysler Historical Collection, Paul C. Curtis, Lanny Knutson, and A.G. Weimann II.

Photo Credits: All photos courtesy Chrysler Historical Collection unless noted otherwise.

Other Photo Credits:

Jim Benjaminson	pp. 70,105-106,111-112
Jim Berka	p. 124
Earl C. Buton, Jr.	p. 49
Collectable Automobile	p. 50
Joe "Whitey" Eberle	p. 85
Art Goddard	pp. 47-48
J. Eric Gould	pp. 28-29
Lanny Knutson	pp. 121-122
William H. Leonhardt	p. 112
State Historical Society of North Dakota	p. 109
Petersen Publishing (Bob D'Oliva)	p. 125
John Rigby	p. 122
Lloyd White Collection	p. 46

Walter Percy Chrysler (1875-1940). The last man to successfully start an automobile company in the United States, Chrysler knew he had to cover all aspects of the industry if his new Chrysler Corporation was going to survive. That included building a full line of automobiles, from the low priced field to luxury models, including a full line of commercial vehicles.

INTRODUCTION

From its inception in the summer of 1928 until the end of production in January 1942, the Plymouth Division of Chrysler Corporation built a confusing array of commercial vehicles - utilizing both passenger car and truck chassis. Despite several half-hearted attempts to enter markets such as the taxi business in its earliest years, it wasn't until 1935 that Plymouth got serious about building commercial vehicles. Even at that point, Plymouth's commercial vehicle production was overshadowed by the offering of rivals Ford and Chevrolet.

Production totals of these various commercial types were not large even when they were new - because of this, their rarity today has caused them to remain virtually unnoticed in the collector car hobby. Most were used - abused - and then discarded, making them among the rarest of Plymouths today.

For the sake of clarity this book will examine the passenger car based commercial offerings first, followed by the truck chassis commercials; photos throughout this book will be divided in much the same manner, although in certain instances there will be a certain mixing of passenger and truck chassis models with similar type bodies.

EARLY COMMERCIAL VEHICLES

Walter Chrysler's entry into the low priced field in the summer of 1928 - as a 1929 model - pitted the four year old Chrysler Corporation against the ranks of America's two largest automakers, Ford and Chevrolet. Offered as a smaller companion to the Chrysler car, the first Plymouth was a conventional four-cylinder automobile. The first commercial offering for the new car was an attempt to crack the taxi market. Although Plymouth maintained a presence in the taxicab market, the majority of the Corporation's taxi sales came from sister division DeSoto. The DeSoto, a larger six-cylinder car on a longer wheelbase, proved itself more practical

for a taxi's need to carry more than the standard number of passengers. By 1932, Plymouth offered a factory built long wheelbase, 7-passenger sedan - something neither Ford nor Chevrolet would ever offer. Many of these were sold to the taxi trade. In later years, despite low sales, a 7-passenger limousine with divider window was cataloged. These vehicles proved popular in the export market, being used in the livery trade overseas.

Plymouth chose the name "Commercial Sedan" to apply to its first sedan delivery in 1930. Built on the four-cylinder 30U chassis, the "Commercial Sedan" was little more than a two-door sedan with a third door added at the rear of the body. Rear quarter windows were blanked out with removable panels. This vehicle was aimed at the small businessman who could afford only one vehicle. With the window panels in place and the rear seat removed, it made the perfect delivery vehicle - especially in areas where real commercial vehicles were prohibited. But on Sundays, with the window panels removed and the rear seat in place, the businessman had a vehicle he could take the family to church in.

Despite its advantages as a dual-purpose vehicle, the "Commercial Sedan" met with little sales success - at $750 it was considerably higher priced than the $565 two-door sedan on which it was based. A mid-year price cut to $675 did little to help - the "Commercial Sedan" was discontinued at the end of the model run after selling just 80 units.

Plymouth advertised a special taxicab on its PA chassis for 1931-1932, but it too saw little sales success. This taxi featured a special interior that seated up to five paying customers - three sitting conventionally in the rear seat, one on a folding jump seat directly behind the driver, with the fifth passenger facing rearward in an alcove alongside the driver. Sales of the $665 taxi special were less than spectacular and it was discontinued after just 112 units had been built. Unique to the taxi was its removable taxi partition and extra seating which "can be replaced with standard sedan seat equipment for resale as a passenger car."

The Commercial Sedan idea would not reappear at Plymouth until 1935; like its predecessor, this vehicle was also based on a converted two-door sedan, in this case, the least expensive flat back two-door. Again, a rear seat was optional. In its work mode, snap-in window blanks covered the rear quarter windows. A single door at the rear offered access to the cargo compartment. The idea of a dual-purpose vehicle had not lost its appeal to Plymouth marketing. Like the 30U Commercial Sedan, it was a vehicle that could be used in the business during the week and as a personal vehicle on the weekend. Priced at $635, this Commercial Sedan saw a production run of 1,142 units.

With the increased acceptance of the Commercial Sedan, Plymouth saw fit to give it its own special body for 1936. No longer the dual-purpose commercial-passenger vehicle, the new commercial sedan had permanently blanked out quarters with a passenger side bucket seat as the only seating option. Based on the P1 Business chassis, the price was reduced by $20 - sales climbed to a record 3,527 units. It should be noted during this period Plymouth used the term "business" to describe its least expensive chassis - thus sales catalogs showed an entire line of body styles carrying the "business" moniker. Buyers of the upscale series got "Deluxe" models. This situation was remedied mid-year 1938 after dealers complained they were losing sales because customers who could not afford the "Deluxe" model balked at being saddled with a "business" car. From then until debut of the 1941 models, the less expensive chassis would be known as the "Road King."

SPECIALTY MODELS

Joining the Commercial Sedan for 1936 were two special purpose options to convert normal passenger vehicles into commercial vehicles. The first, a removable pickup box designed to extend the carrying capacity of the business coupe was cataloged. The pickup box slipped into the trunk opening and could be used with the trunk lid in place or removed. With the pickup box inserted, the lid could not be sealed shut, but it could be locked into place with the tailgate. The pickup box would remain an option through at least the 1939 model year.

The second option first offered in 1936 was the "hearse-ambulance" conversion. For an additional cost of $55, the car body was modified to remove the "X" brace that separated the trunk from the passenger compartment. The rear seat was split and hinged at the center; in normal use the vehicle had a full rear seat. In ambulance mode, half the seat folded and swung up towards the roof of the car, held in place by leather straps. The other half remained in place for the ambulance attendants' use. Patients were loaded headfirst through the open trunk lid - the patients' head and upper torso were inside the passenger compartment proper while the feet and lower extremities remained in the trunk. The ambulance conversion was quite popular with police departments (at that date in time it was the police officers duty to administer to the injured and transport them to a hospital!). The ambulance conversion remained in Plymouth's option books through the 1941 model run. Only during its first year did Plymouth emphasize its hearse capabilities.

Also available on the long wheelbase Plymouths was an ambulance conversion that featured a removable center pillar post on the right side of the vehicle. Held in place with pins and wing nuts, with the doors open and the center post removed, large objects such as gurneys and caskets could easily be placed into the car's interior.

The ambulance conversion could be had only on the P3 and P5 "business" chassis for 1937 and 1938; by 1939 it could be had on either Deluxe or Road King chassis, in either two or four-door models, including the 7-passenger sedan.

OTHER SPECIALTY MODELS

Between the years 1933 and 1940, Plymouth offered, through outside vendors, a line of armor plated vehicles for sale to police departments. The most famous of these was the "Kansas City Hot Shot" - an armor plated 1933 Plymouth purchased by the Kansas City Police Department following the deadly shoot out known as the Kansas City Massacre. Plymouth delivered the basic car to suppliers such as Perfection Windshield or Evans Armored Car of Indianapolis, Federal Laboratories of Pittsburgh or Smart Safety Engineering of Detroit for conversion. Perfection offered four different levels of armament - full body armor added 750 pounds of weight to the vehicle.

STATION WAGONS

Plymouth announced its first wood bodied station wagon on the Deluxe PE chassis for 1934. Like the armor plated Plymouths, the bodies for these cars were supplied by an outside vendor - U.S. Body & Forging. Incomplete cars were shipped to Tell City, Indiana, where U. S. B. & F. installed the bodywork. Once completed, the cars were returned to Plymouth for shipment to the ordering dealer. Even though the wood bodied cars were built on passenger car chassis, they were considered to be commercial vehicles up through 1939 production. The station wagon rode on the commercial truck chassis only one year - 1937. The reason for this may have been due more to a natural disaster than product planning - U. S. Body & Forging's Tell City wagon plant suffered a major disaster from flood waters that year. Production was transferred to Buffalo, New York, where it remained until Plymouth phased out wood body station wagons at the end of the 1950 model year. During this period, the J. T. Cantrell Company of Huntington, Long Island, New York also supplied wagon bodies to Plymouth. Plymouth would also sell bare chassis to those wishing to have custom bodies made by other companies.

LIGHT DUTY COMMERCIAL CARS

Plymouth entered the light duty truck market in 1937 with four body styles built on a truck chassis shared with Dodge. Dubbed the PT series (for Plymouth Truck), body types included the Express (pickup), a cab & chassis (with full-length running boards and rear fenders), Commercial Sedan (sedan delivery) and wood body station wagon. The Panel Delivery would remain on the truck chassis for two years; the wagon for just one.

Reasons for Plymouth entering the light duty truck market were simple. Every Plymouth dealer in both the United States and Canada was dueled with another product from Chrysler. Dodge-Plymouth dealers had a commercial vehicle but those dealers dueled with DeSoto or Chrysler were left without anything to offer prospective buyers. It had to seem like a perfect solution, for little investment, Chrysler Corporation could clone the Dodge pickup and sell it under the Plymouth brand name.

With the economy heating up (1937 would be a banner year for Plymouth, setting sales records that stood until 1950), timing was perfect to enter the light duty truck market.

Built on a 116 inch wheelbase, the 1937 PT50 series Commercial Cars were attractively styled in the manner of the passenger car - although no trim interchanged between the two. Four body styles were cataloged - the Express (pickup), the cab & chassis which continued to come with full length running boards and rear fenders, (a flat face cowl could be ordered for special body applications on special order), the sedan delivery and the station wagon. Standard equipment included safety glass in all windows, a front bumper and single sidemounted spare tire. The pickup box measured six feet long by 47 1/2 inches wide. Power came from a 201 cid valve-in-block 70 horsepower six cylinder engine mated to a three speed transmission (passenger car engines were rated at 82 horsepower).

Changes were minimal for 1938. A shorter, fatter grill matched that of the passenger car. The station wagon returned to the passenger car chassis, cutting the number of PT57 models to three, including the Express, cab & chassis and sedan delivery. Mechanically the PT57 series was carried over from the previous year, with the added option of a four-speed transmission with power take off capabilities.

Plymouth Commercial Cars for 1939 moved away from the passenger car look, taking on a more truck line appearance. Offered in just two models, the Express and cab & chassis (the Panel Delivery moved back to the passenger car chassis) the PT81 series was new from the ground up. Frames were of ladder type construction and wheelbase remained at 116 inches, but all similarities ended there. The cab was moved forward, as was the engine, to provide a larger cargo bed. The PT81 had a modern look with its prowed front end, headlamps mounted on the fender catwalks and a two piece, vee'd windshield. The cab, advertised as a "true three man cab" was claimed to be the biggest offered by any of the "Big Three."

Box size increased to 78 1/8 inches long, with a width of 48 1/4 inches. Mechanically, the PT81 differed little from its predeces-

9

sors. Horsepower remained at 70 from 201 cid with a three-speed transmission standard or four-speed optional.

Minor appearance changes marked the PT105 series for 1940. New were sealed beam headlamps with parking lamps riding in little pods atop the headlamp bucket. The upper grill shell, which had been plain on the 1939 PT81, was treated to the addition of three horizontal stainless steel trim strips. Some PT105 models had the spare tire mounted on the right side of the box, forward of the rear wheel (normal placement for the spare tire was beneath the box).

Mechanical changes to the PT105 included a larger 35-amp generator to handle the sealed beam headlamps and an increase in horsepower to 79. Not seen, but cursed by many, was the switch to left hand and right hand thread wheel bolts. Prices were hiked by $10 - sales increased slightly from the year before.

While the PT81 and PT105 had been very plain, the PT125 for 1941 was quite attractive with its chrome overlay grill patterned after the 1941 passenger car. Stainless steel trim ran in two vertical lines up the radiator shell, divided by a cloisonné emblem. Five horizontal trim strips adorned either side of the center panel. The front bumper, although still painted, had a decided vee in the center. Plymouth nameplates, which previously had been mounted on the radiator shell, moved to the center of the hood panels. The curious looking parking lamp pods of 1940 were replaced by lamps mounted back on the cowl. Most obvious was change of position of the headlamps - now mounted on the crown of the fenders rather than in the catwalks.

Changes had taken place under the hood as well - horsepower was raised to 82, there was a new three-speed synchro-shift transmission and an oil bath air cleaner was made standard. Prices increased by $40 - with a slight drop in production in what would prove to be the last year for a light duty commercial vehicle from Plymouth.

OTHER PASSENGER BASED COMMERCIAL VEHICLES

The Plymouth sedan delivery returned to the passenger car chassis for 1939, as part of the P7 Road King series. It still carried its own special body, now with two rear doors, split vertically. Each rear door contained its own retractable window, with flush mounted handles. A false wooden floor provided a flat load surface offering 124 cubic feet of cargo carrying capacity.

Joining the commercial lineup for 1939 was a vehicle based on the original Commercial Sedan idea of 1930 called the Utility Sedan. Based again on a two-door body, the Utility Sedan was built without a rear seat (a passenger bucket seat was optional), a gutted interior and no partition between the trunk and passenger compartment. An optional screened partition with locking gate was offered.

Unlike the other 1939 passenger cars, the Utility Sedan, Panel Delivery and station wagon carried the spare tire in a fender-mounted carrier.

The Utility Sedan and Panel Delivery for 1940 were mounted on the P9 Road King chassis, although at least one Deluxe P10 Panel Delivery was built to special order. The only noticeable change in the 1940 Panel Delivery was the mounting of the spare tire forward of the right rear wheel. Station wagons, still of all wood construction, were now considered passenger vehicles by the factory.

These same models were carried over into the 1941 model run with only minor trim changes. As 1942 dawned, a new era had taken over at Plymouth. Gone were the ambulance conversion, the Panel Delivery, the Express pickup and the cab & chassis. Left to soldier on by itself was the Utility Sedan. When the last Plymouth rolled out the door January 31, 1942, an era in commercial vehicles came to a close. Like the first Commercial Sedan of 1930, the 1942 Utility Sedan ironically saw the same production total - 80 units.

There were more pressing needs at hand. Detroit was turned into a war machine. President Roosevelt called it the "Arsenal of Democracy." After four long years of war, the automakers slowly got back into the business of making cars to meet a pent up demand unseen before or since. Plymouth didn't need to build any commercial models - it had all it could do to meet the demand for passenger cars.

Introduced in mid-summer 1928, the Model Q Plymouth four-door sedan was soon converted for taxi use. Close examination shows a partition dividing the driver's compartment from the rear seat passengers.

Changes were minimal during Plymouth's first two years of production. Special paint scheme made this 1929 U taxi more distinguishable on the street. Photo Courtesy John Conde.

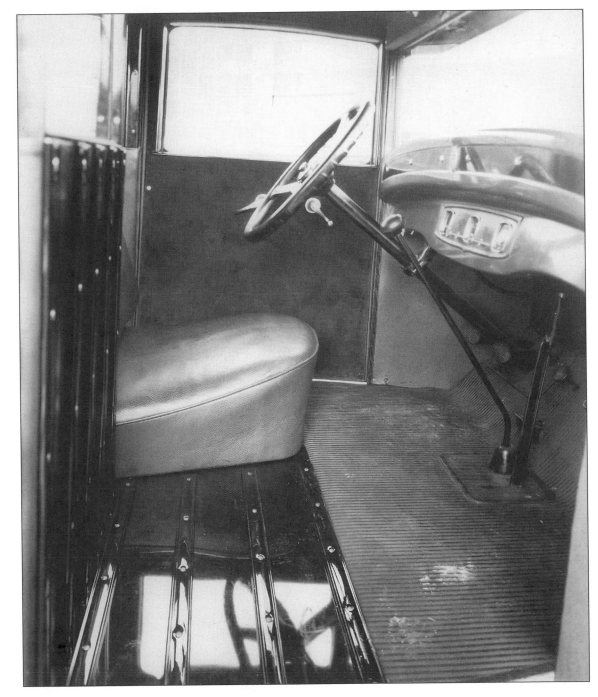

Plymouth taxi drivers faced a rather stark environment.

Rear compartment of the Plymouth taxi was more luxuriously appointed, with mohair upholstery and a foot rail. Rear quarter windows opened for additional air circulation.

PLYMOUTH TAXICAB
LOW PRICED AT $665

a Beautiful Cab

A BEAUTIFUL CAB with a low first cost. Roomy as a car you might pay much more for. Matchless in operating economy.

This cab has the unquestioned economy of a Four—with the smoothness of an Eight. It's the new Floating Power Plymouth chassis. It has Full-pressure Lubrication, Hydraulic Brakes and Safety-steel Body.

Read the long list of quality features. And observe the tremendous popularity of the New Plymouth, being emphasized by car renting companies in their advertising. It pays to use taxicabs of a popular make. Here is a De Luxe Service Cab with an assured profit rate.

AND A LONG PROFIT FOR YOU

Special taxicab folder was issued to promote Plymouth's PA taxi for 1931. At $665 only 112 were sold. Special interior layout featured 5-passenger seating in the rear. One lucky rider got to sit on the folding jump seat, another in a rearward-facing seat in an alcove alongside the driver. Rear seat could still carry three fares. This was the last of Plymouths special taxi models.

By 1939 most of Chrysler Corporations taxi sales were going to the DeSoto Division. However, Plymouth still proved to be popular as a taxicab.

Plymouth for 1940 offered a taxicab accessory package that included a heavy duty clutch, heavy duty shock absorbers and heavier springs - in both the suspension and seat springs. Bumper over riders on this car were not factory supplied.

Udo F. Andres taxi company posed their new 1941 Plymouth taxis for this Christmas greeting. Although Plymouth offered its first two-tone paint schemes on certain 1941 models, these cars carried a company paint layout.

PJ-339

Plymouth built its first 7-passenger sedans in 1932, discontinued them for 1933 and offered them again from 1934 through 1941. Many taxi companies purchased the longer wheelbase vehicles for commercial use. The 1935 PJ Plymouth could be had in two 128 inch wheelbase body styles - a 5-passenger "Traveler Sedan" with built in trunk or a 7-passenger sedan without trunk as pictured here. Only 77 Travelers were built compared to 350 7-passengers.

Long wheelbase 1938 Plymouth could be had only on the Deluxe chassis, again in 7-passenger and limousine form. Wheelbase had increased to 132 inches. Production came to 74 limousines, 1,824 7-passengers with an additional 35 7-passengers specially built as taxicabs.

Wheelbase of the 1939 P8 Deluxe Plymouth 7-passenger increased by an additional 2 inches. Production came to 98 limousines with division window, 1,837 7-passenger sedans plus 12 built specially as taxis.

Wheelbase of the 1940 P10 Deluxe long wheelbase models increased to 137 inches. Being the most expensive models offered, production came to 68 limousines and 1,179 7-passengers. None were specially built for the taxi trade in this year.

1941 P12 Special Deluxe 7-passenger were the last long wheelbase cars built by Plymouth. Wheelbase increased a 1/2 inch over 1940. Production in the final year came to two dozen limousines and 1,127 7-passenger sedans. 1941 would be the first year for two-tone paint schemes.

1941 P12 Special Deluxe 7-passenger sported factory fender skirts and a windshield header mounted radio antennae - it swiveled via a special knob inside the car so the antennae wouldn't get bent when entering a building.

Interior of the 7-passenger featured fold up jump seats that could be folded out of the way when not in use. Comfort level of the jump seats on long trips could be questionable. Automatic courtesy lights were standard on the long wheelbase models. Two-tone interior trim was new for 1941.

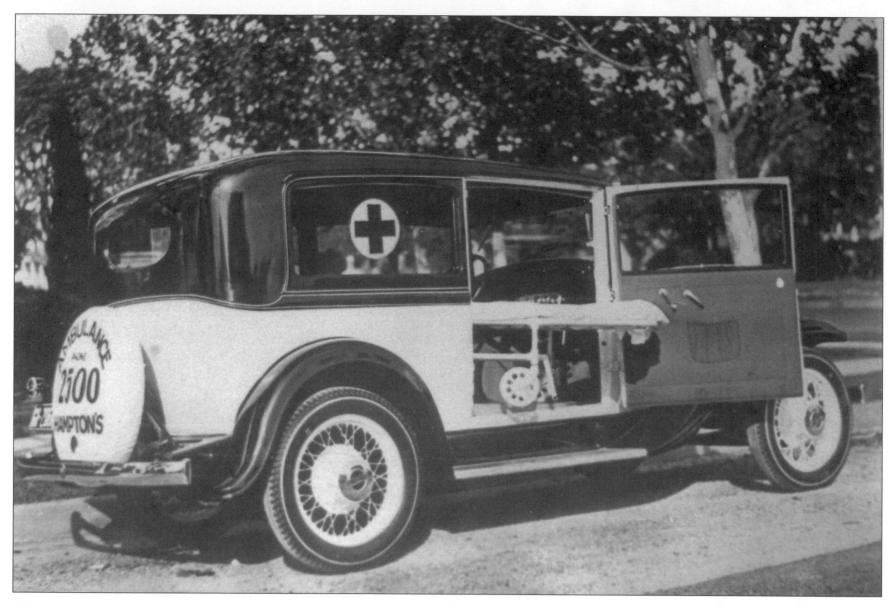

Plymouths were converted for ambulance use as early as 1931. With the seats removed, a gurney could easily be inserted through the passenger door.

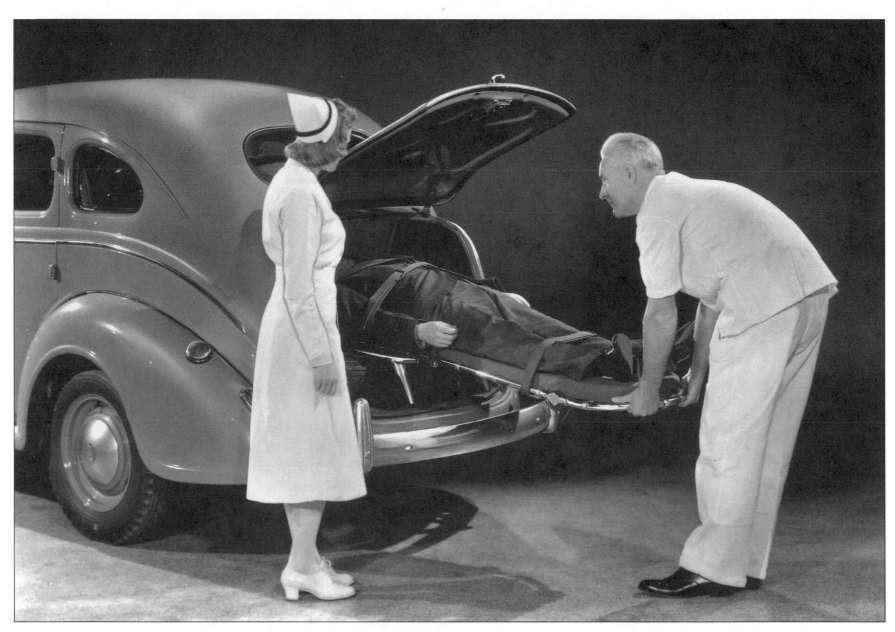

Plymouth offered its first factory built ambulance conversion with the 1936 models. By 1939, the conversion could be had with either two or four doors, but use of the "Touring" model with humpback trunk was mandatory. Conversion cost around $55.

Recently discovered, unrestored ambulance looks like a normal sedan with the doors closed...

Even with the doors open, the car still looks like a normal sedan...

...allows the center post to slip out of place.

Removal of a pin at the base of the pillar post...

Although not regularly cataloged, 7-passenger Plymouths could be purchased with a removable center pillar post for use as a hearse or ambulance.

Top of pillar post is held in place by two pins...

Shows center pillar removed and rear seat slipped out of place.

Interior offers loads of room for a gurney - or casket.

Lack of "X" brace between trunk and passenger compartment also allowed long loads to be inserted through the luggage compartment.

Rear seat of the ambulance conversion was split in half - attendant's seat remained in place while the other half was strapped out of the way against the roof. Hopefully patients weren't claustrophobic as they were inserted into the vehicle!

Gurney had to be inserted over the spare tire in the 1939 ambulance. For reasons unknown, gurney was inserted on opposite sides of the vehicle depending on whether the conversion was built on a two-door or four-door sedan.

Interior view of 1939 Plymouth two-door ambulance put the patient on the left, attendant on the right.

WP-2955

1939 four-door ambulance reversed the seating position of the two-door versions. Leather interior was optional on all models.

Trunk view of 1939 Plymouth ambulance conversion still required gurney to be slid over the spare tire.

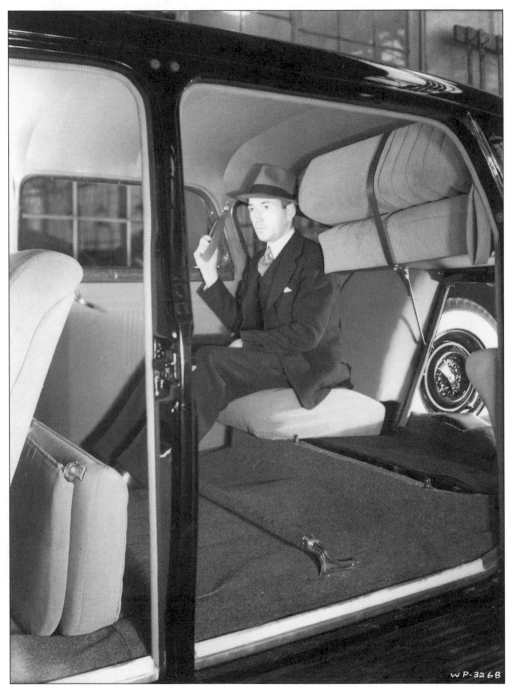

Even the 7-passenger sedan could be built as an
ambulance, shown on this 1940 P10 Deluxe.

WP-3268

Plymouth gave 1939 utility sedan buyers the choice of a flatback body as pictured here, or the humpback style trunk. When converted, the spare tire laid flat on the trunk floor. Ambulance conversions were built only on the humpback "touring" sedan body. It would have seemed far more practical to build ambulances on the sedan delivery, which offered more room for patients and supplies.

Plymouth salesman points out the advantages of the "Police and Industrial Emergency Ambulance" to a prospective customer, this one a 1941 model - the last year the ambulance conversion would be available.

New for 1939 was the P7 Road King Utility Sedan - basically a "gutted" two-door model. Passenger bucket seat was an option, as was the lockable screen cage. 341 Utility Sedans were built, selling for $685.

Utility Sedan was the perfect commercial vehicle to travel where "real" commercial vehicles were prohibited. Rear seat could be fitted at resale time.

WP-3260

Trunk view of the 1940 P9 Road King Utility Sedan shows that the partition normally found between the luggage and passenger compartments could be removed to enable large packages to be carried. Selling for $699, production jumped to 589 units. The Utility Sedan was built through 1942.

From 1936 through 1939, Plymouth offered a removable pickup box that could be fitted into the trunk of the business coupe. Easily installed by one man, the pickup box featured a lowerable tailgate with its own hinged tail lamp that could be plugged into the regular wiring harness. When operated with the tailgate in the open position, the hinged tail lamp hung down to warn oncoming motorists.

Special high clearance wheels were a standard Plymouth option from 1933 through 1941. Sold to those working in oil fields, or to rural mail carriers, wheel size measured 20 inches (vs. 16 inches normally) up through the 1940 model, but was reduced to 18 inches for 1941.

The Plymouth De Luxe 4-door Sedan equipped with "Perfection" bullet-resisting windshield, gun port, bullet-resisting side wings, radiator guards, tire guards. Dash, cowl, headboard, toe-board, and both front door panels are lined with light weight armor steel. In tests made with practically every type of gun known, it has been found that both the glass and steel will stop a bullet from a .45 Thompson Sub-machine gun as well as from the many other types of guns used by practically all bandits. "Perfection" bullet-resisting equipment for Plymouths is sold through authorized Plymouth dealers.

With the Depression Era crime wave of the 1930s, Plymouth found a ready market for armor plated cars for police work. Like the wood body station wagon, Plymouth delivered the car to an outside supplier for the conversion. The Perfection Windshield Company offered several different packages for partial or complete armor plating. Although most of the conversion was under the sheet metal and not seen, visible equipment included radiator, tire guards and a gun port through the bullet proof windshield. This 1935 PJ "Perfection" Plymouth was delivered to the Sioux Falls, South Dakota police department following a raid on the local bank by the John Dillinger gang.

NET PRICE LIST ON
"PERFECTION" BULLET-RESISTING EQUIPMENT for POLICE CARS

(New prices effective January 1, 1935)

	Net Price to Police Dept. or Sheriff	Confidential Dealers' Net Price
Bullet-Resisting One-Piece Windshield Complete with Special Frame	$80.00	$67.50
Bullet-Resisting 2-Piece or Divided Windshield Requiring 2 Frames	87.50	75.00
Bullet-Resisting Gun Ports, including installation in glass	27.50	22.50
Bullet-Resisting Side Wings, per pair	62.50	50.00
Bullet-Resisting Radiator Guard	82.50	70.00
Bullet-Resisting Tire Guards, per pair	50.00	40.00
Armor Dash, Cowl, Toe- and Head-Board with Special Bullet-Resisting Steel	110.00	90.00
Armor Both Front Doors with Special Bullet-Resisting Steel	50.00	40.00

Prices quoted f. o. b. Indianapolis, terms fifty per cent cash-with-order, balance upon delivery.

The above prices are subject to a two per cent Federal Tax, unless we are furnished with a letter or affidavit from dealer stating that this equipment is being purchased for use on a police automobile, upon which the dealer holds a bona-fide order.

Dealers can make installation of Windshield, Side Wings, Radiator and Tire Guards. We must have car in our shop to armor Dash, Cowl, Toe- and Head-Board and Front Door Panels. When Radiator Guards are shipped to dealer it will be necessary for dealer to furnish us with regular radiator shell to build front into it. We will make installation of any of the above equipment at no additional cost to dealer if car is delivered to our shop.

We are in a position to completely armor any automobile to any extent desired. Prices upon request. Prices subject to change without notice.

PERFECTION WINDSHIELD COMPANY
INDIANAPOLIS, INDIANA

Price sheet for armor plating the 1935 Plymouth from the Perfection Windshield Company of Indianapolis.

Armor plated 1938 P5 Road King was delivered to the LaPorte, Indiana police department. Note the machine gun poking through the gun port of the windshield.

Long after the gangster era of the mid-1930s, armor plated Plymouths were still proving popular with law enforcement. This 1940 P9 Road King was used by the Alcohol Beverage Control unit of Edgecomb County, North Carolina.

Prior to the United States entry into World War II, Plymouth built 2,028 1941 P11 Deluxe four-door sedans specifically built for use as military staff cars. Pictured here at the Aberdeen Proving Grounds in Maryland, changes from regular Plymouth sedans included olive drab paint, painted over chrome trim and the addition of black out lamps above the regular headlamps. Hubcaps dated from 1938.

Plymouth began selling wood body station wagons in 1934, calling it the Westchester Semi-Sedan Suburban. Chassis were shipped to the U. S. Body & Forging Company for installation of the body. Up through 1939 Plymouth considered the station wagon to be a commercial vehicle. Although just 35 were sold the first year, production climbed to 309 units when this 1936 model was built. It sold for $765.

Belt molding of contrasting red gum was a trademark of the U. S. Body & Forging Company bodies. Tail lamp on this 1936 Westchester is not original.

Several changes occurred in Plymouth's 1937 wagon lineup. Production of the wagon - and sedan delivery - was moved to the new PT50 truck chassis. A disastrous flood at the Tell City, Indiana plant, where wood bodies were built, caused production to be moved to Buffalo, New York. During this time period, the J. T. Cantrell Company of Huntington, Long Island, New York also built wagon bodies for Plymouth. This is the only known example of a 1937 PT50 Westchester with body by Cantrell. Wagon production increased to 602 units, which sold for $740.

Station wagon production returned to the passenger car chassis for 1938. Although 555 1938 Westchesters were built, just two of the $880 wagons are known to have survived.

Plymouth gave buyers of its 1939 P8 Deluxe station wagon a choice in window treatments. For $940, the wagon came with curtains across the rear quarters and tailgate, or for an additional $30, glass in all windows.

1939 would be the last year Plymouth passenger vehicles could be had with fender mounted spare tires - and then only on the sedan delivery, station wagon and utility sedan. Wagon production jumped to 1,680 P8 Deluxe units with an additional 97 built for export sales on the P7 Road King chassis.

1940 P10 Deluxe wagon production jumped to 3,126 units while still selling for $970. An additional 80 wagons were built on the P9 Road King chassis for export sales.

Plymouth wagon building techniques remained basically the same from 1934 through 1948. Because of the unique nature of the construction of wood bodies, these photos show the intricate details required for their restoration.

Split rear window is a distinctive feature at the rear of the wagon. Note the hinged tail lamp, so it can hang down when the vehicle is operated with the tailgate in the lowered position.

Tailgate is held in the horizontal position by retaining braces on either side. Note the skid strips on the inside surface of the tailgate.

While the tailgate has two braces, the lift gate has just one to hold it in the open position.

Wagons came with three rows of seats - the two rear sets removable and interchangeable, although one seat is narrower that the other. Normally the narrowest seat would be in the number two position, making it easier for rear seat passengers to get into the vehicle.

With the rear seat removed, the wagon could still carry five passengers, plus cargo.

Placement of the spare tire is obvious in this photo now that the second seat has been removed. Note the tail lamp in its lowered position with the tailgate open.

Spare tire located behind the front seat robbed rear seat passengers of some legroom. Note the recess in the floor for the tire to fit into. Upholstery was leather.

Rear compartment, with the two rear seats removed, left plenty of room for cargo or luggage.

Intricate woodwork was kept in place with screws and metal braces. Tailgate mechanism looks fairly complicated.

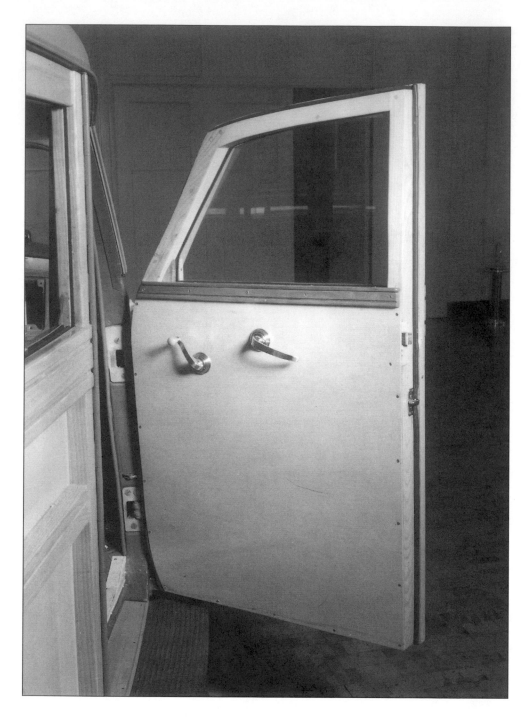

Even the interior door panels were wood. Door and window handles were special to the station wagon, featuring longer shanks.

Purchasers of the 1941 P12 Special Deluxe station wagon were given the option of two-toned woodwork at no additional charge. The wood body was framed in white ash with the buyer's choice of white maple or Honduras mahogany paneling. Wagon production jumped to 5,594 units, selling for $995. An additional 217 wagons were built on the P11 Deluxe chassis for sale to export markets.

The last prewar Plymouth wagon was this 1942 P14C Special Deluxe of which only 1,136 were built before production shut down on January 30, 1942. Prices had jumped to $1,145. This would be the first (and last year) that a Plymouth wood body station wagon had full-length stainless trim on the body. Most chrome trim was eliminated early on, resulting in what historians today call "black-out" models. Just two 1942 Plymouth wagons are known to exist; only one of which carries a factory body.

After an experimental entry into the commercial field with the 30U Commercial Sedan, Plymouth again decided to offer the body style on the PJ series chassis for 1935. It was based on the flat back two-door sedan, with a door added at the rear of the body.

1935 PJ Commercial Sedan sold for $635, $100 over the two-door sedan which it was based on. Production came to 1,142 units.

PJ Commercial Sedan could easily be converted into a passenger car when needed. Window blanks were removable and a rear seat could easily be slipped into place. Even the rear quarter windows rolled down.

One of the few restored 1935 PJ Commercial Sedans has been fitted with PJ Deluxe trim, including fender skirts and whitewall tires. Right hand fender mounted spare tire was standard, while a left sidemount fender was optional.

Showroom display of the 1936 P1 Commercial Sedan showed off the new body, which was no longer based on a passenger vehicle. The fender mounted spare tire features the optional metal tire cover, but the radiator ornament is the standard (and export) type - compare it to the more familiar sailing ship ornament found on the car parked behind the commercial sedan.

Like its earlier brethren, the 1936 Commercial Sedan had a single door at the rear - with a roll down rear window. Sales jumped to 3,161 units, no doubt helped by a $30 price decrease over 1935.

Gasoline filler cap was located inside the rear door of the Commercial Sedan.

Interior of the 1936 sedan delivery was spartan. Note the dash is not wood grained; all gauges were centered in the dashboard.

Interior of the 1936 sedan delivery provided acres of cargo capacity. Sidewalls were now covered in a Masonite type paneling - seat upholstery was in gray "leather like" material.

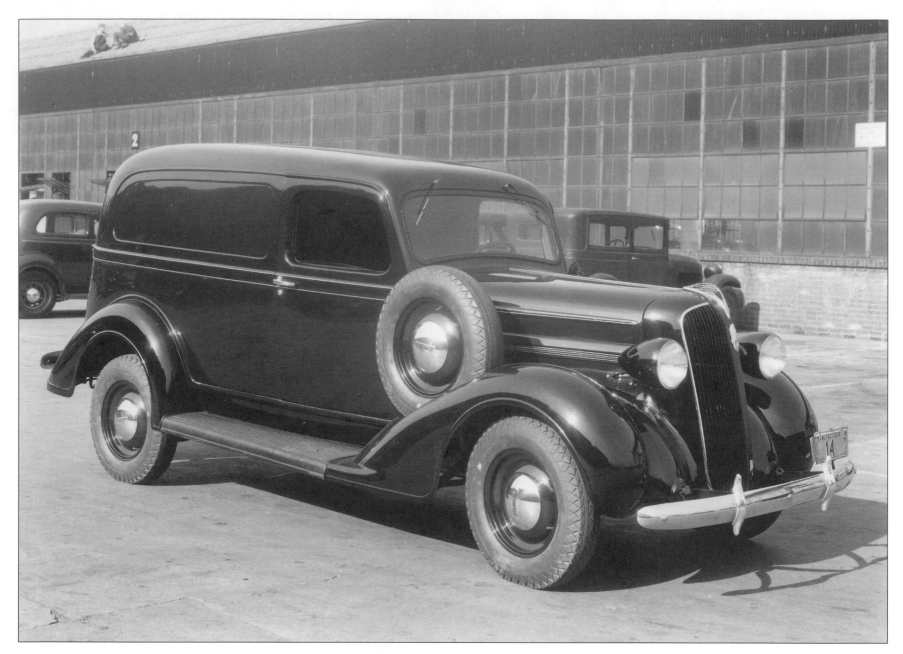

Plymouth moved the sedan delivery to the PT50 truck chassis for 1937. The ll6 inch wheelbase was a 3 inch increase over previous years.

Once again, a single rear door, with roll down rear window was standard equipment. Prices were hiked to $655, but a booming economy raised demand for the sedan delivery to 3,256 units.

We don't know what our two fearless hunters are after, but there is plenty of room to haul their catch in the back of their 1937 PT50 sedan delivery.

National Conservation Bureau

TRANSCONTINENTAL TOUR for TRAFFIC SAFETY

HARVARD UNIVERSITY—Driver Training Safety Education Bureau
for Street Traffic Research— Cooperating

Automobile Furnished by PLYMOUTH MOTOR CORPORATION

WP·2162

Plymouth provided this PT50 sedan delivery to Harvard University's driver education safety tour. The vehicle was driven coast to coast under the auspices of the National Conservation Bureau's Transcontinental Tour for Traffic Safety.

Finding a restored Plymouth sedan delivery at a car show is a daunting task. This is one of the few restored examples in the country, a 1937 PT50 displayed at Hershey.

Few changes were made to the sedan delivery for 1938. Once again, it rode on the truck chassis, now coded PT57. A price increase to $695, coupled with a sharp recession, saw sales fall to 1,601 units.

Plymouth decided to return the sedan delivery to the passenger car line for 1939, this time on the P7 Road King chassis. Buyers snapped up 2,270 of the $715 vehicle.

Fender mounted spare on the 1939 "Panel Delivery" would mark the last time Plymouth would locate the tire in that location. Although these fenders could fit all 1939 Plymouth passenger cars, they were only used on the sedan delivery, station wagon and utility sedan.

With the return to the Road King chassis for 1939, Plymouth decided two rear doors were more convenient than one to reach the 124.6 cubic feet of cargo space. Each door still had a roll down rear window.

Restored example of the P7 Road King Panel Delivery displayed at a Plymouth Owners Club national meet.

1940 Road King based Panel Delivery saw a slight increase in sales to 2,846 units - prices were increased $5 over 1939.

1940 P9 Panel Delivery was equipped with many factory accessories, including wheel trim rings, bumper guards and twin spotlights.

Although the Panel Delivery was based on the Road King chassis, factory records show one was built on the Deluxe P10 chassis to special order. This is probably that vehicle - built as a mobile studio for a radio station. This P10 version featured a full-length belt line molding of stainless steel and mounted the spare tire on the left side of the body.

Right side of the P10 Deluxe Panel Delivery special featured steps up the right side leading to a padded rooftop, apparently so reporters could stand on the roof of the vehicle to get a better view.

Interior of the P9 panel differed little from earlier years. The driver still sat on a bucket seat.

The idea behind the original Commercial Sedans of 1930 and 1935 had been to sell one vehicle to fit two purposes. For 1940, Plymouth called its sales force together to promote the "See One, Sell Two" program. The idea was for the salesman to visit one customer and sell him two vehicles - a passenger vehicle for his personal use and a commercial vehicle for his business.

In its last and final year, the 1941 Panel Delivery was built on the P11 Deluxe chassis. Full-length body side moldings added a little flash to the otherwise spartan looking vehicle.

Sales of the 1941 P11 Panel Delivery came to 3,200 units, just 21 shy from the record set in 1937 for that body style. Panel Delivery retailed for $745.

Rear view of the 1941 P11 panel shows the two rear doors and single tail lamp - rear windows were now fixed in place as they had been since 1940.

1940 and 1941 Panel Delivery carried the spare tire in an indentation on the right side of the vehicle.

Little changed from previous years - the 1941 Panel Delivery offered plenty of cargo capacity in a stylish, passenger-based vehicle.

The Two Way Control Plymouth Drop Frame Delivery Car was an early concept commercial vehicle tested by the company. Close examination reveals the Plymouth was really a Dodge.

Dodge saw respectable sales of its humpback delivery sedan as early as 1933 - one has to wonder how many Plymouth deliveries of this style could have been sold had it been offered.

Plymouth's entry into the light duty pickup market was this 1937 PT50 Express. Buyers had their choice of a complete unit as shown here or a cab & chassis only.

Sales of a record 10,709 Express pickups reflect the robust economy of 1937. Fender mounted spare tire on the right side was standard, but the buyer paid extra for a matching spare on the left.

Frontal appearance of the 1937 PT50 was similar to that of the 1937 passenger car, but nothing was shared between the two except the front bumper.

Rear bumper on the PT50 was optional - and quite rare today. Note the weights in the box of this Express - they were placed there to give the vehicle a lowered appearance in publicity photos. Another photographers trick was to chain the springs down to achieve the same look.

Workmen in the factory put the finishing touches on a PT50 Express as it nears the end of the line before being shipped to a dealer. Note the front bumper is wrapped in paper to protect it during shipment. Once on the showroom floor, the Express retailed for $525. A cab & chassis unit (of which 158 were built) sold for $495.

The 1938 PT57 Express was changed just enough to match its passenger counterpart. Again, nothing interchanged except the front bumper. A deep recession in 1938 saw sales fall to just 4,620 Express and 95 cab & chassis units. Prices had increased substantially to $585 and $560 respectively, which didn't help sales any.

Restored 1938 PT57 at a Plymouth Owners Club National Meet.

Highly prized by restorers is the Plymouth script tailgate as found on this PT57.

Completely redesigned for 1939, the PT81 Express featured a larger cab and box, although the wheelbase was the same as the 1937-1938 pickups at 116 inches.

Nearly devoid of bright trim, only the nameplates, hubcaps and radiator molding were chrome. The front bumper was painted aluminum. Note this truck has the optional dual windshield wipers - a single, vacuum powered wiper was standard. Adding a vacuum wiper for the passenger side cost an additional $4. For $6 the driver could enjoy an electric wiper - dual electric wipers retailed for $13.

Ulmen Motors of Bismarck, North Dakota delivered 100 of the 6,181 1939 PT81 Express pickups built to the federal government. Retail price was $575, although we doubt the government paid that much for them. (Andreas Risem photo courtesy State Historical Society of North Dakota)

1939 PT81 cab & chassis came with full-length running boards and rear fenders. 140 customers shelled out $545 for this combination.

It took a sharp eye to detect the differences between the 1940 PT105 Express over the PT81. Prices rose $10 across the board. Production rose to 6,879 Express and 179 cab & chassis units.

The addition of three bright moldings to the radiator shell, plus the parking lamp pods atop the headlamp shell were the only visible differences between 1939 and 1940. Sealed beam headlamp system was an industry wide change for 1940.

Fender mounted spare tires had been eliminated with the change to the new larger body style in 1939. Plymouth opted instead to place the spare in a carrier beneath the box. Some - but not all - PT105 models carried the spare on a special carrier forward of the right rear fender. This was the standard spare tire mount for Dodge military vehicles - and it's possible those Plymouth pickups with the sidemount carrier were originally destined for military or government use.

Special rear fender with a tire indentation and mounting arm riveted to the frame rails was required to carry the spare in this location.

Rear bumper was optional, as was the right hand tail lamp. Buyers also had the choice of a plain or script tailgate. The tailgate on the 1939 through 1941 Plymouth pickups is slightly larger than that of the 1937-1938 pickups.

Built only as a prototype was this 1940 PT105 Plymouth command car. As the nation edged ever closer to war, Dodge began supplying the military with various special bodies. By the time war came, all production was centered on models bearing the Dodge nameplate.

The 1941 PT125 Express would be the last pickup Plymouth would build. Selling for $625, the Express would see a production run of 6,073 units - an additional 196 cab & chassis units sold for $590.

Overall view of the PT125 made it easy for the observant to pick out the styling changes over previous years. Most noticeable was placement of the headlamps on the crown of the fender, vee'd front bumper, addition of cowl lamp parking lamps and moving the Plymouth nameplates from the radiator shell to the hood sides.

Using the same sheet metal as previous years, Plymouth stylists came up with an overlay featuring stainless brightwork accented by paint stripes and horizontal grill bars similar to that used on the 1939 and 1940 Plymouth passenger cars.

Although most Plymouth pickups came in solid colors, purchasers could opt for "painted sheet metal," which normally included black fenders, running boards and splash aprons. If the body color was dark blue, the radiator shell was also painted black.

Spare tire was carried in a holder beneath the pickup box. Tailgate could be had with or without script name - right hand tail lamp was a $2.50 option.

Close up look at the under box spare tire carrier reveals it is the same as that found on many later day pickups.

By the end of the 1941 model run, all of these commercial vehicles would be gone from the Plymouth sales lineup, with the exception of the Utility Sedan, which would soldier on for one more year. Sales of the 1941 P11 Deluxe Utility Sedan came to 468 units, selling for $739 - the same price as the two-door sedan on which it was based.

A factory worker looks on as a 1941 P11 Panel Delivery makes its way down the line where it will be mated to its chassis.

Chrysler Canada also offered a companion line of commercial vehicles, badged under the Fargo nameplate. It made its appearance one year earlier than the Plymouth Commercial Cars and lasted until 1972. Unlike Plymouth, which could only be had in half ton form, Fargo's could be had up to three ton capacity. Pictured here is a 1946 one ton Fargo with 9-foot box.

Fargo used the same sheetmetal as the Plymouth. 1946 Fargo carried the same bright trim as the 1941 PT125 Pickup.

Fargo's were built in both Canada and the United States - the U.S. built models were shipped to export markets with the exception of Mexico, where the same truck was badged as a DeSoto!

DeSoto nameplate was used on Dodge cloned vehicles long past the demise of the DeSoto marque in the United States - seen here as a 1959 Town Wagon.

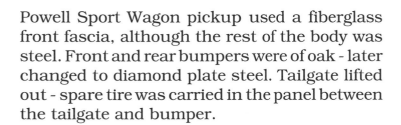

Although not related to Chrysler Corporation, the Powell Sport Wagon has a unique place in Plymouth history. The Powell Brothers, Channing and Hayward, began producing a line of "recycled" pickups - mounting their own bodies on rebuilt 1941 Plymouth chassis.

Powell Sport Wagon pickup used a fiberglass front fascia, although the rest of the body was steel. Front and rear bumpers were of oak - later changed to diamond plate steel. Tailgate lifted out - spare tire was carried in the panel between the tailgate and bumper.

The only "new" car on the market to sell for under $1,000, Powell production began in 1955, lasting into early 1957. 1941 Plymouth chassis were obtained from a local wrecking yard. After removal of the original body, the chassis was rebuilt before the Powell's installed their own bodies. Power came from rebuilt Plymouth, Dodge and Chrysler Industrial six cylinder engines. The Powell's added a station wagon late in the 1956 model year. Each car was sold with the then standard new car guarantee of 30 days or 4000 miles, with service available at any Chrysler dealership.

Unique to the Powell Sport Wagon was the optional 7 inches wide, 6 feet, 6 inches long "Utility Tray" designed for carrying fishing rods, rifles and other long objects. Vehicle could be had without the tray; when one tray was ordered it was fitted to the right side of the vehicle. Prices for 1956 rose to $1,195 for the standard model - $1,295 for the Deluxe, which included signal lights, two-tone nylon upholstery, chrome trim on the bodyside and grill, a single Utility Tube and rear bumper with standard trailer hitch. Wagons commanded $1,675.

Tailgate of the Powell Sport Wagon was hinged at the roofline and lifted in one piece. Rear of the wagon provided sleeping for two adults. An optional pop-up camper top was cataloged for the pickup.

Powell Sport Wagons were built in Compton, California - total production is thought to have been around 1,500 pickups and 300 station wagons.

More Titles from Iconografix:

This product is sold under license from Mack Trucks, Inc. Mack is a registered Trademark of Mack Trucks, Inc. All rights reserved.

All Iconografix books are available from direct mail specialty book dealers and bookstores worldwide, or can be ordered from the publisher. For book trade and distribution information or to add your name to our mailing list contact

Iconografix   Telephone: (715) 381-9755
PO Box 446   (800) 289-3504 (USA)
Hudson, Wisconsin, 54016   Fax: (715) 381-9756

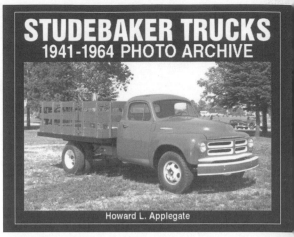
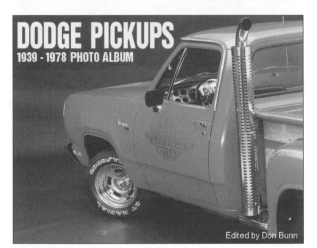
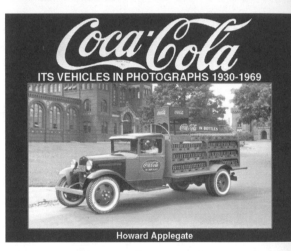
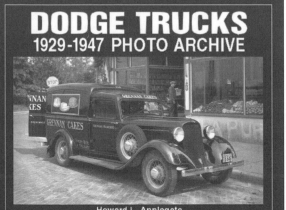